PRINCIPLES OF BUSINESS – by TINA A SM

UNIT 3 – D/506/1942

Level 3

Credit Value 10 - 74GLH

Content:

Outcome 1 Understand business Markets

1.1 Explain the characteristics of different business markets

1.2 Explain the nature of interactions between businesses within a market

1.3 Explain how an organisation's goals may be shaped by the market in which it operates

1.4 Describe the legal obligations of a business

Outcome 2 Understand business innovation and growth

2.1 Define business innovation

2.2 Explain the uses of models of business innovation

2.3 Identify sources of support and guidance for business innovation

2.4 Explain the process of product or service development

2.5 Explain the benefits, risks and implications associated with innovation

Outcome 3 Understand financial management

3.1 Explain the importance of financial viability for an organisation

3.2 Explain the consequences of poor financial management

3.3 Explain different financial terminology

Outcome 4 Understand business budgeting

4.1 Explain the uses of a budget

4.2 Explain how to manage a budget

Outcome 5 Understand sales and marketing

5.1 Explain the principles of marketing

5.2 Explain a sales process

5.3 Explain the features and uses of market research

5.4 Explain the value of a brand to an organisation

5.5 Explain the relationship between sales and marketing

1.1 Explain the characteristics of different business markets

Perfect competition

A perfectly competitive market is a hypothetical market where competition is at its greatest possible level. Neo-classical economists argued that perfect competition would produce the best possible outcomes for consumers, and society.

Key characteristics

Perfectly competitive markets exhibit the following characteristics:

There is perfect knowledge, with no information failure or time lags. Knowledge is freely available to all participants, which means that risk-taking is minimal and the role of the entrepreneur is limited.

There are no barriers to entry into or exit out of the market.

Firms produce homogeneous, identical, units of output that are not branded.

Each unit of input, such as units of labour, are also homogeneous.

No single firm can influence the market price, or market conditions. The single firm is said to be a *price taker*, taking its price from the whole industry.

There are a very large numbers of firms in the market.

There is no need for government regulation, except to make markets more competitive.

There are assumed to be no externalities; that is no external costs or benefits.

Firms can only make *normal* profits in the long run, but they can make abnormal profits in the short run.

The firm as price taker

The single firm takes its price from the industry, and is, consequently, referred to as a *price taker*. The industry is composed of all firms in the industry and the market price is where market demand is equal to market supply. Each single firm must charge this price and cannot diverge from it.

In the long run

However, in the long run firms are attracted into the industry if the incumbent firms are making supernormal profits. This is because there are no barriers to entry and because there is perfect knowledge. The effect of this entry into the industry is to shift the industry supply curve to the right, which drives down price until the point where all super-normal profits are exhausted. If firms are making losses, they will leave the market as there are no exit barriers, and this will shift the industry supply to the left, which raises price and enables those left in the market to derive normal profits. The super-normal profit derived by the firm in the short run acts as an incentive for new firms to enter the market, which increases industry supply and market price falls for all firms until only normal profit is made.

Evaluation

The benefits

It can be argued that perfect competition will yield the following benefits:

Because there is perfect knowledge, there is no information failure and knowledge is shared evenly between all participants.

There are no barriers to entry, so existing firms cannot derive any **monopoly power**.

Only normal profits made, so producers just cover their opportunity cost.

There is no need to spend money on advertising, because there is perfect knowledge and firms can sell all they can produce. In addition, selling unbranded goods makes it hard to construct an effective advertising campaign.

There is maximum possible:

Consumer surplus

Economic welfare

There is maximum allocative and productive **efficiency**:

Equilibrium will occur, hence allocative efficiency.

In the long run equilibrium will occur, which is productive efficiency.

There is also maximum choice for consumers.

How realistic is the model?

Very few markets or industries in the real world are perfectly competitive. For example, how homogeneous is the output of real firms, given that even the smallest of firms working in manufacturing or services try to differentiate their product.

Although unrealistic, it is still a useful model in two respects. Firstly, many primary and commodity markets, such as coffee and tea, exhibit many of the characteristics of perfect competition, such as the number of individual producers that exist, and their inability to influence market price. Secondly, for other markets in manufacturing and services, the model is a useful yardstick by which economists and regulators can evaluate levels of competition that exist in real markets.

Taken from
http://www.economicsonline.co.uk/Business_economics/Perfect_competition.html

---

Imperfect competition is a competitive market situation where there are many sellers, but they are selling heterogeneous (dissimilar) goods.

Definition: Imperfect competition is a competitive market situation where there are many sellers, but they are selling heterogeneous (dissimilar) goods as opposed to the perfect competitive market scenario. As the name suggests, competitive markets that are imperfect in nature.

Description: Imperfect competition is the real world competition. Today some of the industries and sellers follow it to earn surplus profits. In this market scenario, the seller enjoys the luxury of influencing the price in order to earn more profits.

If a seller is selling a non-identical goods in the market, then he can raise the prices and earn profits. High profits attract other sellers to enter the market and sellers, who are incurring losses, can very easily exit the market.

There are four types of imperfect markets:
- Monopoly (only one seller) - Oligopoly (few sellers of goods) - Monopolistic competition (many sellers with highly differentiated product) - Monopsony (only one buyer of a product)

Taken from

http://economictimes.indiatimes.com/definition/imperfect-competition

In Conclusion -

A perfect competitive market does not exist in the real work only in theory, as there are too many influencing factors to consider. The idea for a perfect market would see that all sellers are open and honest about all trading and transactions that all products are equal and un- branded, with equal pricing in any retail outlet, unable to change the pricing as this would be set across the whole market – can you imagine this in the real world? Phones as a typical example: no branding – all the same – all having the same features, and all at the same price. Would this not then become a non-competitive market?

Would this then mean that If I brought a phone from Tesco I could return it to Sainsbury – as it would be no different – would we even need to have different shops – if they were all to be the same – we would not need Tesco, Sainsbury, Waitrose, Aldi, Adsa, they could all merge into one big hypermarket with no need for branding we could name them by department instead – food, clothing, electrical.

Whereas the imperfect competition sees the market in a realistic view of the world, where all competitors are able to influence the retail pricing due to their buying power, or their unique product.

Monopoly (only one seller) - A single company or provider has absolute control over the supply that is released into the market, giving that particular provider the ability to dictate prices. In the absence of any competition, the lone seller is free to keep prices high, without fear of being undercut by another provider. This would be highly unfavourable for consumers, as it gives them no recourse to seek alternatives that might force prices lower. The regulating bodies, such as the Department of Justice - have made it difficult for one supplier to monopolize the market, as they enforce antitrust laws that help promote free trade. As an example any corporate merger would have to be checked out by the DoJ first to make sure that it would not create an unfair market. This would also be measured against the Herfindahl-Hirschman Index, which is a calculation that measures the degree of concentration in any given market and is one tool that regulators use to support them in their decision making process.

Oligopoly (few sellers of goods) - An oligopoly is a **market structure** in which a few firms dominate. When a market is shared between a few firms, it is said to be highly concentrated. Although only a few firms dominate, it is possible that many small firms may also operate in the market. For example, major airlines like **British Airways** (BA) and **Air France** operate their routes with only a few close competitors, but there are also many small airlines catering for the holidaymaker or offering specialist services.

Monopolistic competition (many sellers with highly differentiated products) – Monopolistic competition is where production does not take place at the lowest possible cost. Because of this, firms are left with excess production capacity. The four main points of monopolistic competition are:

1. All firms produce similar yet not perfectly substitutable products.

2. All firms are able to enter the industry if the profits are attractive.

3. All firms are profit maximizes.

4. All firms have some market power, which means none are price takers.

Monopsony (only one buyer of a product) – This is a market similar to a monopoly except that a large buyer, not seller controls a large proportion of the market and drives the prices down. This has also been known as "the buyer's monopoly". As an example of this:

People have accused Ernest and Julio Gallo (the big wine makers) of being a monopsony. They had such power buying grapes from growers, that sellers had no choice but to agree to their terms.

The last part was taken from
http://www.investopedia.com/terms/m/monopsony.asp

1.2 Explain the nature of interactions between businesses within a market

In a perfect competition market

Many consumers will buy a product that is standard across the board from many businesses. The prices would be set and consumers would pay one price for the product from any business. Therefore the business would have to rely on its reputation and customer service for the sales of a product, as opposed to the price or reduction it would be able to offer the consumer.

In an imperfect market

Monopolies – all consumers would buy from a set product from one business and that business would set the price and would be the only business to offer that product.

Monopolistic competition – consumers would have a choice of very similar but not the same products from different businesses – for example basic products in Sainsbury verses value products in Tesco. These businesses will offer competitive prices and demand for that product would affect the price.

Oligopoly – an economic condition in which there are so few suppliers of a product that one supplier's actions can have a significant impact on prices and on its competitors.

Monopsony – the consumer would have autonomy over prices and be able to dictate the price to the business selling the product. A situation in which a product or service is only bought and used by one customer

1.3 Explain how an organisation's goals may be shaped by the market in which it operates

Perfect Competition

Although this is a theoretical market there are some unique markets that operate under these conditions in which a product is traded freely by buyers and sellers in large numbers without any individual transaction affecting the price. Therefore the goals of this organisation would be to sell in volume offering excellent customer service and SLA (service level agreements) maximising profits and achieving growth and expansion into the impact competitive market. It would look to increase market shares, profitability, sales in volume and also value, as well as expanding the product range on offer. The organisation would hope to influence the product pricing and the consumer choice.

This organisation would be looking to maximise profits, sales volume and value, growth and profitability. Increase the market share, the power it has in the market over other, competition. The organisation would also be looking to achieve a state of monopoly with a product or become an oligopoly – where the market would be dominated by very few sellers. This organisation would want to satisfy the stakeholder and achieve a return on capital employed.

DEFINITION of 'Return On Capital Employed (ROCE)'
(http://www.investopedia.com/terms/r/roce.asp)

This is a financial ratio that measures a company's profitability and the efficiency with which its capital is employed. Return on Capital Employed (ROCE) is calculated as:

ROCE = Earnings before Interest and Tax (EBIT) / Capital Employed

"Capital Employed" as shown in the denominator is the sum of shareholders' equity and debt liabilities; it can be simplified as (Total Assets – Current Liabilities). Instead of using capital employed at an arbitrary point in time, analysts and investors often calculate ROCE based on "Average Capital Employed," which takes the average of opening and closing capital employed for the time period.

A higher ROCE indicates more efficient use of capital. ROCE should be higher than the company's capital cost; otherwise it indicates that the company is not employing its capital effectively and is not generating shareholder value.

Overall the market factor for both imperfect and perfect competition is with supply and demand, in the market place. They will look at costing for products and revenue, as well as looking at profits, and flexibility in the market. The organisations overall goal is to maximise profits, maximise sales by volume, offering the best SLA and customer satisfaction, to please stakeholders and increase market shares.

Business structure

A quick comparison of the different trading structures available, with more detail to help you decide which option will be best for you.

Sole Trader

Limited Company

Partnership

Social Enterprise

Compare different trading structures

Once you've made up your mind that you are going to start in business you need to decide what form the business will take. Each of the following options has its own merits and limitations.

TYPE OF STRUCTURE	BUSINESS METHOD	RESPONSIBILITIES	ACCOUNTS	TAX STATUS
SOLE TRADER - Probably the simplest solution if you want to start up on your own. There's less paperwork and fewer formalities than partnerships & limited companies	You run the business and make the decisions.	You are individually responsible for any debts and obligations that the business owes.	You don't have to produce a balance sheet or have accounts audited.	You need to let the tax authorities know that you are starting in business as your tax status will change to self employed.

PARTNERSHIP - Know as much as possible about your prospective business partner to help avoid any unwelcome surprises later on	You will be liable as an individual for any debts or obligations incurred on behalf of the firm by your partner(s) even if you did not agree or know what transaction they had entered into.	It makes sense to draw up a partnership agreement which formally documents the arrangements between the partners - your solicitor can do this for you.	You don't need to produce accounts, but it would be wise to do so.	Each partner will be taxed separately on their share of the drawings from the business.

LIMITED COMPANIES - More complex than setting up as a sole trader or a partnership.	Limited Companies are legal entities in their own right, distinct from the directors who run them. This means that as a Director your liability for debt will be limited to the capital you have invested in the business (except where you have granted personal	Limited Companies are bound by Companies Act legislation.	The company's secretary and directors have legal duties Example: prepare audited accounts and make an annual return filing these accounts at Companies House within the timescales set down by law.	Directors are classed as employees for income tax purposes

	security/ guarantees for the company's obligations).			
SOCIAL ENTERPRISE- Setting up your business to trade on the internet this can be done as a SOLE TRADER or LIMITED COMPANY	You run the business and make the decisions. See above	You are individually responsible for any debts and obligations that the business owes. See above	You don't have to produce a balance sheet or have accounts audited. See above	You need to let the tax authorities know that you are starting in business as your tax status will change to self employed.
Taken from http://www.uk.parkerrandall.com/what_we_do/start-ups_advice/business_structure				

Understand basic legal requirements

The rules and regulations around company names

Choosing a name for your company is a long-term decision. You will want your name to encapsulate, in a few memorable letters or words, precisely what it is you're selling or offering. And it will take many years to build your name up in the consciousness of your customers. So you want to make sure you get it right at the outset.

If you're forming a limited company, you won't be able to register a name which is considered the same as that of an existing company, or one which could be considered offensive or illegal.

There is a range of rules you will need to bear in mind. You can also get free advice on business names from Companies House.

Trademarks, copyrights and patents

A trademark identifies your product specifically in the eyes of the public, and when registered, is protected by law, giving you the right to take action against anyone else using it. Similar rules apply to copyrights and patents which exist to protect the fruits of your hard work against rival businesses and others using them without your permission. Unlike patents, which must be applied for, copyrights happen automatically. Again, your solicitor can advise you in this area.

Staying on the right side of the trading laws

There are certain laws, such as the Trades Description Act and Sale of Goods Act, which were drafted specifically to protect the consumer. You must be mindful of these laws and adhere to them.

Trading laws exist for your protection, too, so it is important that you have at least a basic understanding of the law and how it affects your business. You can find out about the trading laws from your solicitor and there are also various books on the subject.

What insurances are legally required?

You should view insurance as a necessity, and a major priority for your business. There are some insurance that the law demands you have, and others which you should take out as a matter of your own protection. You must have employers' liability insurance, motor insurance (where appropriate), insurance demanded by any contracts you may have, and insurance for certain types of engineering equipment.

Understanding your tax liabilities

Putting business expenses down against your gross profit reduces the amount of tax you will have to pay. That is why keeping accurate records is so important. Professional advice from an accountant will ensure that your tax obligations are met. Also, the Inland Revenue can deal with your queries direct.

The issue of VAT usually sends shivers down the spines of most small businesses. In effect, you act as tax collector for the Government, collecting indirect taxes on goods bought from you and passing the money on to Customs and Excise. The main thing to remember about VAT is to keep accurate records at all times.

'Should I register for VAT' is the title of the official guide on the subject which can be obtained from the Department of Trade and Industry. Or you can ask your accountant or local VAT officer for advice.

2.1 Define business innovation

- This is the art of creating, a process of inventing or introducing something new in the business environment.

- The development of a new product or service

- A new way to increase profitability

- A new way to improve business efficiency

- New ideas

- Adding value to services, and / or products

- Looking to offer a USO - A unique service offer is one that differentiates the offer that an organisation is making from that of its competitors or comparable organisations.

2.2 Explain the uses of models of business innovation

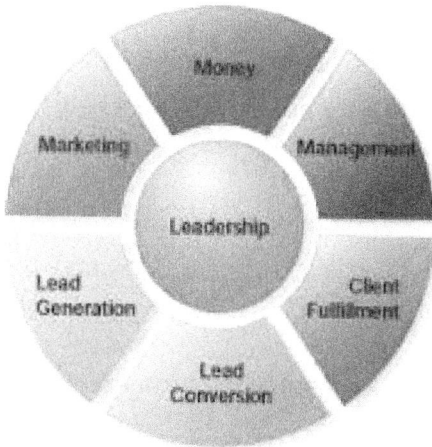

The Seven Centers of Management Attention™
Business Success Model

There are many different business models used at different stages of business creation, the model above show the key elements within any business:

- Money

- Management

- Client fulfilment

- Lead Conversion

- Lead Generation

- Marketing

- Leadership

In this example above we could place any values we needed to create a new model.

The business might look at which industry it operates in and whether it could be creative and move into a new industry or even create a new industry in which to operate.

Within another model there may be a revenue plan – looking at new ways to create sales and move into other areas of business. They may also look at strategic planning and pricing models.

The business may also look at networking, expanding the business or competitive suppliers.

They may look at restructure within the business and innovative marketing.

An example of this would be the Cadbury advert with the gorilla playing the drums – who would have thought that something so different would be remembered for so long.

This awesome Cadbury commercial from 2007 was an instant classic. It featured a gorilla playing the drums to "In the Air Tonight" by Phil Collins and is as impressive, funny, and entertaining as anything we've ever seen. Great marketing stands out and this commercial certainly stands out.

http://vimeo.com/62839747

Internally the company may have a marketing section that would complete research in the market and analyse sales trends and availability. Other support and guidance within the business would come from Directors, Management, stakeholders, workshops, customer service department, training and workshops run by head office to encourage innovation within teams.

Externally the company could bring in experts in their field, advertising companies, partnerships, networking, website design and marketing, different trading events, support from trade bodies, various industry groups, the government.

Product development goes through 8 stages these are:

Stage 1.   Hold brainstorming sessions, SWOT analysis, market research, customer feedback, Analysis of possible competition in the market.

Stage 2.   Who is the target market? Is the idea conceptual? Analysis market trends, find out what competitive pressures there are, what is the profit on the product?

Stage 3.   Identify and intellectual property issues, what are the features? What are the benefits? What will the consumer reaction be? Analysis production costs

Stage 4.   Analyse positional selling prices, estimate sales volumes, analyse break-even point looking at production costing and supply and demand. Market trends, logistically positioning of entry to the market

Stage 5.　　　Prototype produced, tested and feedback analysed, test packaging design and introduce at trade shows, complete pilot studies and distribution channels

Stage 6.　　　Estimate resources required and the cost involved, create operation plans, publish any technical data, and resource plan, finalise supplier agreements, logistics plan and make sure that contingency plans are in place.

Stage 7.　　　Product launch activities are planned, promotional materials created and published, advertising activities are finalised, there is a critical path analysis and the distribution pipeline is finalised

Stage 8.　　　Analyse customer reaction, analyse consumer value, price, and demand, production costs analysis, review forecasted sales volumes, revenue and profit, review after sales service, analyse the impact of the new product against the existing portfolio of similar products.

Benefits that are associated with innovation are:

- Improved customer experiences

- Smarter ways to work

- Improving brand reputation

- Improved products / services

- Business growth / expansion

- Increased recognition

- Being able to offer unique service

- Improved processes

- Develop new markets

- Open niche market

Risks that are associated with innovation are:

- Failing to meet Quality

- Production costs

- Scheduling

- Resources

- Demand

- Predicted sales

- Return on investment

As well as this there may be internal factors such as resistance to change, unsupportive staff, or unclear procedures or unsupportive systems in place.

Implications that are associated with innovation are:

- Employee training and skills

- Attitude to change

- Perception

- Stakeholders collaboration

- Corporate strategy

- Corporate social responsibility

3.1 Explain the importance of financial viability for an organisation

Financial viability is the ability of an organization to continue to achieve its operating objectives and fulfil its mission over the long term. Things that are considered here are resources, if they are adequate, cost effective and fit for purpose, staff levels and any plant, machinery and logistics. Facilities and administration along with working capital, determine solvency, looking at maintaining and increasing profitability. Cash flow and investments can be maintained or increased. Planning for the future is in place with some form of marketing strategy in place for long term business goals. A 5 year or 10 year plan for financial, as well as physical growth of the company is in place and on target to achieve.

3.2 Explain the consequences of poor financial management

Lack of financial planning or poor control over finances would overall cost the company money and maybe place them into insolvency.

Financial management

The cycle of financial management is a repetitive one and missing out or misinterpretation of any one of these would become a disaster. A typical example of this is Tesco, who thought they had more money than they actually had when they reported their financial data this year

Analyse – is the business in line with the business plan? Are there variances? Is the business in line with the budget? What are these variances? What are the sales figures? What is the marketing plan? Analyse resources, assets, planning, cash flow, wastage, theft, problems in the business, policies and processes, risk analysis, legal obligations, employee's skills and training, competition. There are possible many more areas to analyse, but this gives an overall look at different areas that that to be reviewed regularly.

Budget – looking at the sales and expenditure of the company, looking at maximising the profits and still have the ability to invest. Some analysis from above will be considered in this area as well. Management in this area is critical and budgeting for each department and other areas within the business has to on target and contingency plans should be in place for support within each department.

Reporting – when all analyse is completed for any given timeframe there are reports, these can be daily reports, weekly, monthly, half yearly and annually. All areas of the business will be using reports of some form, including those on the shop floor, looking at daily figures on sales and running comparison reports on figures against last week, last month, and last year. All in line with supporting the overall business plan – looking at current market trends that may have affected sales and outside influences that are out of the company control. For example bad weather, power cuts, and flooding will all have an impact on a business and that business needs to be prepared for that impact and where it will take them, if they have a contingency in place then they will be prepared.

Assets – looking at the resources and the property that the company owns. Identify the need for that and analyse the best use of it. for example should the company have a plane / or planes for their corporate clients and how often would this be used – can this company do without this asset – or it is for use not only as a commercial tool, but as a status symbol that the company is doing so well, that they can afford to have their corporate clients and Directors flying around in a plane or planes? On the other side, maybe looking at how many stores are open, how many do they plan to open and by when, what equipment to they need, when do they need it by and is their cash flow consistent and are they in line with corporate long term business plan.

Resource Allocation – staffing levels and allocation of material to site across the company including logistics dependant on schedule. There are many resources allocation models this lone below is a very simple one.

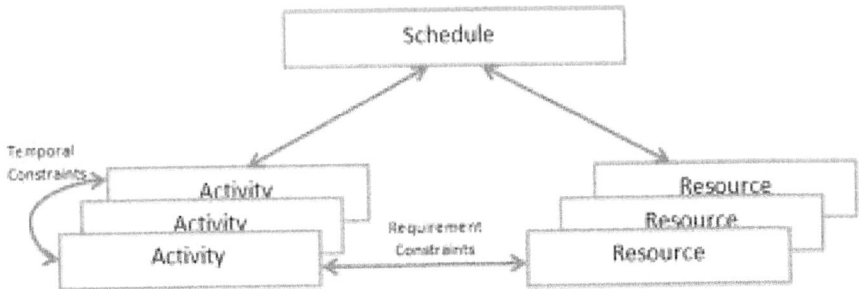

3.3 Explain different financial terminology

Accounts

Financial transactions conducted through an account of financial records, of an organization that register all financial transactions, and must be kept at its principal office or place of business. The purpose of these records is to enable anyone to appraise the organization's current financial position with reasonable accuracy. Firms present their annual accounts in two main parts: the Balance Sheet, and the income statement (profit and loss account). The annual accounts of a registered or incorporated firm are required by law to disclose a certain amount of information. And have to be certified by an external auditor that they present a 'true and fair view' of the firm's financial affairs.

Accruals

Accounts on a balance sheet that represent liabilities and non-cash-based assets used in accrual-based accounting. These accounts include, among many others, accounts payable, accounts receivable, goodwill, future tax liability and future interest expense

Assets

Assets that have a physical form. Tangible assets include both fixed assets, such as machinery, buildings and land, and current assets, such as inventory. The opposite of a tangible asset is an intangible asset. Nonphysical assets, such as patents, trademarks, copyrights, goodwill and brand recognition, are all examples of intangible assets.

Balance Sheet

A financial statement that summarizes a company's assets, liabilities and shareholders' equity at a specific point in time. These three balance sheet segments give investors an idea as to what the company owns and owes, as well as the amount invested by the shareholders

Break-Even Point

The point at which gains equal losses

Capital

"Capital" can mean many things. Its specific definition depends on the context in which it is used. In general, it refers to financial resources available for use. Companies and societies with more capital are better off than those with less capital.

Cash flow

A revenue or expense stream that changes a cash account over a given period. Cash inflows usually arise from one of three activities - financing, operations or investing. Cash outflows result from expenses or investments.

Creditors

An entity (person or institution) that extends credit by giving another entity permission to borrow money if it is paid back at a later date.

Debtors

A company or individual who owes money

Depreciation

A method of allocating the cost of a tangible asset over its useful life. Businesses depreciate long-term assets for both tax and accounting purposes.

Expenditure

Funds used by a company to acquire or upgrade physical assets such as property, industrial buildings or equipment. This type of outlay is made by companies to maintain or increase the scope of their operations. These expenditures can include everything from repairing a roof to building a brand new factory. Also known as Capital Expenditure or "CAPEX"

Fixed Costs

A cost that does not change with an increase or decrease in the amount of goods or services produced. Fixed costs are expenses that have to be paid by a company, independent of any business activity. It is one of the two components of the total cost of a good or service, along with variable cost.

Gross Profit

A financial metric used to assess a firm's financial health by revealing the proportion of money left over from revenues after accounting for the cost of goods sold. Gross profit margin serves as the source for paying additional expenses and future savings.

Income

A company's total earnings (or profit). Net income is calculated by taking revenues and adjusting for the cost of doing business, depreciation, interest, taxes and other expenses. This number is found on a company's income statement and is an important measure of how profitable the company is over a period of time. The measure is also used to calculate earnings per share.

Investments

A business unit that can utilize capital to directly contribute to a company's profitability. Companies evaluate the performance of an investment centre according to the revenues it brings in through investments in capital assets compared to the overall expenses.

Liabilities

A company's legal debts or obligations that arise during the course of business operations. Liabilities are settled over time through the transfer of economic benefits including money, goods or services. Liabilities include loans, accounts payable, mortgages, deferred revenues and accrued expenses. Liabilities are a vital aspect of a company's operations because they are used to finance operations and pay for large expansions. They can also make transactions between businesses more efficient.

Net Profit

A percentage that is paid out of the working interest owner's share of net profits.

Profit and Loss Account

A financial statement that summarizes the revenues, costs and expenses incurred during a specific period of time - usually a fiscal quarter or year. These records provide information that shows the ability of a company to generate profit by increasing revenue and reducing costs. The P&L statement is also known as a "statement of profit and loss", an "income statement" or an "income and expense statement".

Shares and Stock

Most stocks are traded on physical or virtual exchanges. The New York Stock Exchange (NYSE), for example, is a physical exchange where some trades are placed manually on a trading floor (other trading activity is conducted electronically). NASDAQ, on the other hand, is a fully electronic exchange where all trading activity occurs over an extensive computer network, matching investors from around the world to each other at the blink of an eye.

Investors and Traders

These submit orders to buy and sell stock shares, either through a broker or by using an online order entry interface (i.e., a trading platform such as E*Trade). A buyer bids to purchase shares at a specified price (or at the best available price) and a seller asks to sell the stock at a specified price (or at the best available price). When a bid and an ask match, a transaction occurs and both orders will be filled. In a very liquid market, the orders will be filled almost instantaneously. In a thinly traded market, however, the order may not be filled quickly or at all.

Physical Exchange

At a physical exchange, such as the NYSE, orders are sent to a floor broker who, in turn, brings the order to a specialist for that particular stock. The specialist facilitates the trading of a given stock and maintains a fair and orderly market. If necessary, the specialist will use his or her own inventory to meet the demands of the trade orders.

Electronic Exchange

On an electronic exchange, such as NASDAQ, buyers and sellers are matched electronically. Market makers (similar in function to the specialists at the physical exchanges) provide bid and ask prices, facilitate trading in a certain security, match buy and sell orders, and use their own inventory of shares, if necessary.

Tax

Five major types of business taxes are:

(1) Corporate franchise tax,

(2) Employment (withholding) tax,

(3) Excise tax,

(4) Gross-receipts tax,

(5) Value added tax (VAT).

Some types of firms (such as insurance, mining, and petroleum extraction companies) pay additional taxes peculiar to their industries.

While firms too, pay income, property, and sales taxes, such taxes are not specific to businesses.

Transaction

An economic event that initiates the accounting process of recording it in a company's accounting system. The events that affect the finances of a business and must be recorded on the books. Transactions are recorded in what are known as "journal entries." Each entry describes a single transaction and states its date and amount.

Turnover

In accounting, the number of times an asset is replaced during a financial period. The number of shares traded for a period as a percentage of the total shares in a portfolio or of an exchange

Variable Costs

A corporate expense that varies with production output. Variable costs are those costs that vary depending on a company's production volume; they rise as production increases and fall as production decreases. Variable costs differ from fixed costs such as rent, advertising, insurance and office supplies, which tend to remain the same regardless of production output. Fixed costs and variable costs comprise total cost.

VAT

A type of consumption tax that is placed on a product whenever value is added at a stage of production and at final sale. Value-added tax (VAT) is most often used in the European Union. The amount of value-added tax that the user pays is the cost of the product, less any of the costs of materials used in the product that have already been taxed. Indirect tax on the domestic consumption of goods and services, except those that are zero-rated (such as food and essential drugs) or are otherwise exempt (such as exports). It is levied at each stage in the chain of production and distribution from raw materials to the final sale based on the value (price) added at each stage. It is not a cost to the producer or the distribution chain members, and whereas its full brunt is borne by the end consumer, it avoids the double taxation (tax on tax) of a direct sales tax. Introduced by the European

Economic Community (now the European Union) in the 1970s.

Read more:

http://www.businessdictionary.com/definition/business-tax.html#ixzz3HuKMSxbX

The main point of a budget is to plan your finances, and be able to adapt accordingly.

This is a comprehensive evaluation of an investor's current and future financial state by using currently known variables to predict future cash flows, asset values and withdrawal plans.

Most individuals work in conjunction with an investment or tax professional and use current net worth, tax liabilities, asset allocation, and future retirement and estate plans in developing the plan. These will be used along with estimates of asset growth to determine if a person's financial goals can be met in the future, or what steps need to be taken to ensure that they are.

The things that would be reviewed here are:

- Incoming and expenditure
- Targets and objectives of the business growth
- To provide direction
- To assign overall responsibilities

- Monitor and review KPI

- Planning of future activities and growth

- Support innovation

- Training for staff

To manage a budget first you must understand what money is available and how much money has to be spent in order to maintain your department / business / company.

Firstly you need to identify your priories and timescales. What resources you need and any contingency plans. As there may well be unforeseen circumstances in which you may need alternative or extra resources and staff. Allowing also for outside influences such as bad weather, power cuts and flooding – all of which you cannot control.

You will need to accurately record all incoming and out goings. Analyse and monitor these against the plan.

Here is an example:

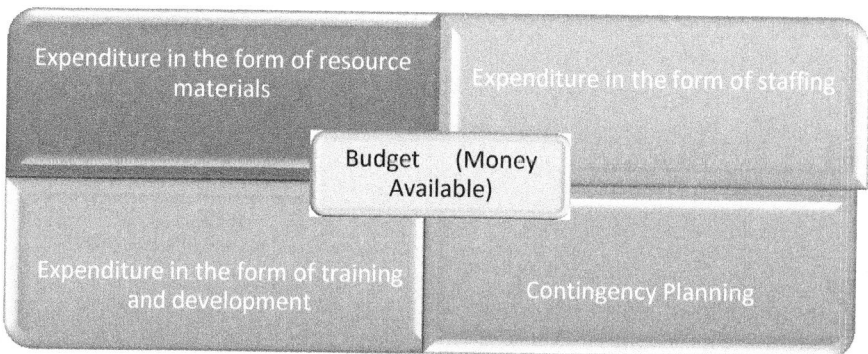

Expenditure in the form of resource materials	Expenditure in the form of staffing
Budget (Money Available)	
Expenditure in the form of training and development	Contingency Planning

If we place this into financial terms –

| £1000 per calendar month for Department A | → | Staffing for 1 month costs £400 | → | Resources for month cost £300 | → | training and development cost £100 | → | total these all up £800 | → | therefore leaving £200 for contingency / emergency funding |

This is only a very basic model to give an understanding within a department – obviously within the company's accounting department this is on a much larger scale and more detailed.

5.1 Explain the principles of marketing

This involves a range of processes concerned with finding out what consumers want, and then providing it for them

The 7P's of marketing are:

Marketing

- Product
- Price
- Place
- Promotion
- People
- Physical Presence
- Process

- Product – Appearance, features, packaging, longevity warranty

- Price – must be priced correct – and in line with any competition on the market

- Place – must be available, in shops in line with advertising

- Promotion – advertising will support and increase sales

- People – those responsible for the marketing and advertising campaigns

- Physical Presence – how the consumer will view the product, packaging, staff knowledge, service offered, branding, organisation

- Process – delivery to customer

5.2 Explain a sales process

Seven Step Sale Process

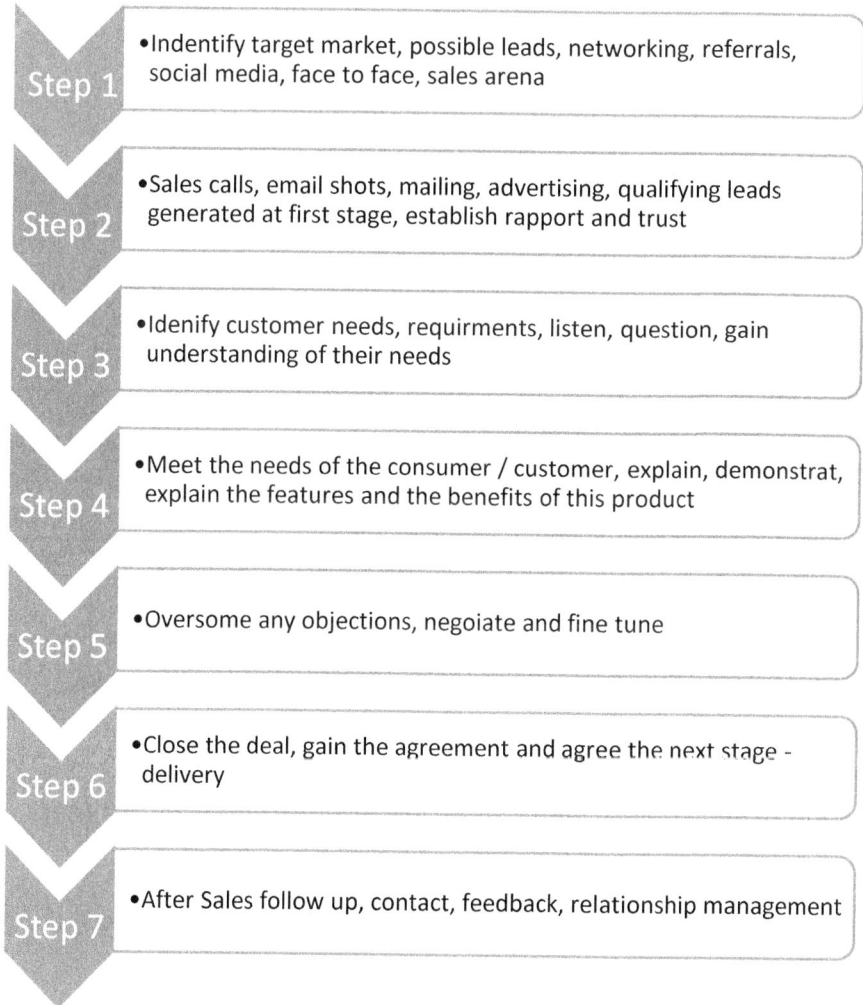

Step 1
- Indentify target market, possible leads, networking, referrals, social media, face to face, sales arena

Step 2
- Sales calls, email shots, mailing, advertising, qualifying leads generated at first stage, establish rapport and trust

Step 3
- Idenify customer needs, requirments, listen, question, gain understanding of their needs

Step 4
- Meet the needs of the consumer / customer, explain, demonstrat, explain the features and the benefits of this product

Step 5
- Oversome any objections, negoiate and fine tune

Step 6
- Close the deal, gain the agreement and agree the next stage - delivery

Step 7
- After Sales follow up, contact, feedback, relationship management

Features

The features of market research are:

- Customer comments and feedback
- Word of mouth (is free advertising)
- Comment cards
- Surveys
- Questionnaires
- Recommendations

Quality research - Qualitative research is designed to reveal a target audience's range of behaviour and the perceptions that drive it with reference to specific topics or issues. It uses in-depth studies of small groups of people to guide and support the construction of hypotheses.

The results of qualitative research are descriptive rather than predictive

- Quantity research – used in the following situations:

- New product idea generation and development

- Investigating current or potential product/service/brand positioning and marketing strategy

- Strengths and weaknesses of products/brands

- Understanding dynamics of purchase decision dynamics

- Studying reactions to advertising and public relations campaigns, other marketing communications, graphic identity/branding, package design, etc.

- Exploring market segments, such as demographic and customer groups

- Studying emotions and attitudes on societal and public affairs issues

- Assessing the usability of websites or other interactive products or services

- Understanding perceptions of a company, brand, category and product

- Determining consumer language as a preliminary step to develop a quantitative survey

- Primary research leading onto secondary research –

Primary research is defined as factual, first-hand accounts of the study written by a person who was part of the study. The methods vary on how researchers run an experiment or study, but it typically follows the scientific method. One way you can think of primary research is that it is typically original research.

Secondary research is defined as an analysis and interpretation of primary research. The method of writing secondary research is to collect primary research that is relevant to a writing topic and interpret what the primary research found. For instance, secondary research often takes the form of the results from two or more primary research articles and explains what the two separate findings are telling us.

Uses

The uses of marketing research are the following:

- To be able to measure behaviours within a consumer group
- Trends in sales
- Buying patterns
- Success of product development
- Competitive activities
- Brand awareness
- Reputation
- Changes in the market
- New market openings

- New technologies
- New social trends
- Politics
- Economy
- Legalities
- Test new ideas

The value of a BRAND to an organisation would be a unique selling point, giving competitive advantage. The name, logo, image, design, and / or symbol, would be considered to reflect the company image and culture to the audience market. Therefore the customer will associate that Brand with that company and recognise it for value, quality, service, and benefits.

As an example – Costa Coffee – their logo here – showing coffee beans - people immediately think coffee, quality brand, quality coffee, good snacks and cakes available, collect points to use in other sites. They have been around since 1971, so therefore well established. The opportunity to give feedback via their website and check your points on your card, they also send out promotion emails offering extra points of free cakes when purchasing a new blend of coffee. During the summer they have many varieties of smoothies as well. They are a subsidiary of Whitbread. Whitbread has 7 branded subsidiaries including Premier Inn hotel chain. They have also seen the benefits of incorporating many Premier Inn hotels with a lounge area offering Costa Coffee. Also some sites do not have in house restaurants' but do have a Brewers Fayre or a Beefeater Grill near to their hotels and these are also part of Whitbread. This is one of those companies who have clearly marked out their brands and clearly see the value of this.

5.5 Explain the relationship between sales and marketing

Sales and marketing have been in different departments since the beginning of business. With the latest technologies, including sales force and marketing automation, the gap between sales and marketing is decreasing. When the two functions come together, communication barriers are broken and ultimately if done correctly, revenues increase.

Even though marketing and sales are two very different functions within a company, one cannot survive without the other. Both bring different assets to an organization as a whole. The inherent connection between the two lies in the fact that they share a similar goal: increasing revenue. Marketers generate leads and sales executives close the deal. Both sales professionals and marketers, however, need to work in order to nurture their leads. Because they share this mutual objective, the means in which they accomplish this should complement each other.

The positive relationship will encourage open communication, planning together, common objectives within a multitalented team of both Sales and Marketing; they should consult with each other and share client relations. They are after all working towards the same shared goal of creating revenue, growing the business and increasing business innovation. Between the two teams they will have more knowledge of the consumers' needs, available to them and improved production and development within the teams.

Between them the goal is to increase sales and gain feedback that they can use to create unique creative and memorable advertising. The draw back here is if the team are of variant mind sets and not will to co-operate with each other. Then lack of communication, and trust will inhibit the communications, with conflicting goals, constrained product development and lack of innovation, motivation and responsibility.

CPSIA information can be obtained
at www.ICGtesting.com
Printed in the USA
LVOW04s1700281015

460129LV00027B/1027/P